Have you ever ...?

Compiled by
Robert J. Smith

For more information or to order additional copies, please contact:

LGT Family Church
288 Commissioners Rd. W.
London, ON   N6J 1Y3
1 (519) 685-1920
Email: info@lgt.org
www.lgt.org

Printed in Canada
by Bannerman Publishing
www.bannermanpublishing.com

Please visit www.bannermanpublishing.com for a new inspirational daily proverb or to find information on other publications and other Christian authors.

DEDICATION

This book is dedicated to so many who have been wounded. Your pain should touch all our hearts, to encourage and help you in your difficult journey.

In our society we find so many wounded people. Many are wounded in their bodies and need help on a daily basis just to survive. Others are wounded in their emotions or souls; for them, putting the past behind is very difficult, and for some, almost impossible. There is always hope if we know where to go for help. Then there are those who are wounded in their spirit, which is where people need to make things right with God. The place to begin to have our wounded spirit restored is to ask God's Son, Jesus, into our hearts and ask Him to forgive our sins and restore our broken lives.

Jesus can bring healing and restoration into our spirit, soul and body if we ask Him. As you read the stories in this book, I trust you will be blessed as you hear how others found the help they needed.

HAVE YOU EVER...?

ACKNOWLEDGEMENTS

I would like to express my sincere appreciation to all those who have shared their personal stories for this book. Sometimes to reveal the innermost part of ourselves can be a big challenge. The individuals in this book have graciously opened up their hearts and lives to share intimate stories with us. The driving force behind this is that somehow through their experiences, those who read this book may find some hope, guidance and inspiration to be empowered in their own lives to take steps of faith and find personal freedom.

A special thanks to Ruth Moore for all her hours of editing and assistance with writing some of the stories. Also, to Tena Moore for coordinating and putting the book together.

INTRODUCTION

Crisis moments cross the path of life for all of us. In our daily walk, so many find a journey that they never expect.

As an eighteen year old young man I was driving my dad and brother to a New Year's Eve celebration in Montreal. A drunk driver hit our car and my dad died in my arms. In a matter of minutes, my life unexpectedly changed forever. To me it looked like a total disaster, but God walked me through it. I had a personal faith in Jesus Christ that sustained me during the desperately difficult days that lay ahead.

When I look back, I realize that out of a terrible accident, God was still able to bring good things into my life.

In this booklet, I have asked several people who have had desperate crisis situations in their lives to share their stories. The common theme in all the stories is that they found help through their personal faith in Jesus Christ.

While everyone's story is unique and painful, they have all found hope for their future.

I trust that you will be encouraged and find a personal faith in God and hope through what they have shared.

Robert Smith
Senior Pastor, LGT Family Church

Lorraine's Story

As a single working woman, I found that I was often lonely and depressed. I see now that I should not have felt that way since I had heard and understood the good news about Christ's purpose on earth. I had accepted God's gift of spiritual life and should have been happy. However, due to my life circumstances, I was mad at God because I was alone.

My life changed significantly one day when I discovered 'the lump'. It was a miracle that I found it and somehow I knew instantly that it was cancer. God took over from there. Within ten days I was diagnosed with an aggressive form of cancer. My life was no longer in my control.

Within a month of finding the lump, I had it surgically removed along with my lymph nodes. I am grateful that I was lifted up and supported by family and my spiritual leaders during this time and I found myself feeling the presence and protection of angels. I was lovingly and gently led through a deep valley when I was desperately trying to not lose hope. I was struggling to find joy.

I am so thankful that God provided me with the best of doctors and medical treatment. I believed that the surgery got all the cancer; nonetheless I knew that I would still need chemotherapy and radiation. I began to realize that with the help of God I would get through this.

During my ten months of treatment, daily I read Psalm 91 from my Bible. I hung on to those words. They were personal to me; *"He is my refuge and my strength, there shall be no harm come to you, He shall give His angels charge over you. I will satisfy you with long life."*

> "Within ten days I was diagnosed with an aggressive form of cancer. My life was no longer in my control."

During my time of treatment my life was dramatically changed. God did an amazing work in me! My faith was strengthened daily. I learned so much! I learned to be thankful in everything. I learned to rest and 'be still' in Him. I learned to receive from others, as God showed me that He would provide everything that I needed.

Since then I have been blessed with a strong faith in the healing powers of the Almighty One. *"Don't you know that your body is the temple of God and you are not your own? You are bought with a price. God is in your body and in your spirit"* (I Corinthians 6:19, 20). I needed this assurance and it showed me that I am important, loved and as special as anyone else.

Since my recovery my life is different and so much better. I am constantly reminded that my life is in His hands. I am aware that when my thoughts become negative I need to give thanks always as I am reminded of what God has done for me. Emotionally I know that He wants me to have JOY always. I give it all to Him; I trust and have no need to worry. My thoughts and attitudes have been so important to my healing. **Every day is a gift.** God has restored my body and blessed me with new strength, both physically and spiritually. I have new hair, new nails, new eyebrows, new eyelashes and new friends. My finances have been restored and I am filled with hope. Daily I hang on to God. I value worship time with Him as well as time to be still with Him.

I look at Psalm 23 verse 3; *'He renews my strength. He guides me along right paths, bringing honour to His name'.* Now I have been blessed with the opportunity to be a member of a National Championship Breast Cancer Survivor Dragonboat Racing Team. Now I have been blessed with the promise of a God-loving spouse and family. Now I have been blessed with a faith to pray for the sick and those going through cancer treatments. Now I have been blessed with the opportunity to share with other women in a support group for cancer survivors and those dealing with cancer. The group is called 'CELEBRATE LIFE!' and is part of the ministry of LGT Family Church.

I owe it all to Him. Praise be to God!

Katie, Nancy and Megan's Story
as told by Katie

It is odd how you can remember the details of certain days in your life; what you were wearing, what you ate, certain smells and the exact words that were spoken. It was on such an unforgettable day that my family learned some of the worst news imaginable. The only problem was... we heard it twice.

My family consists of six people, relatively large by today's standards. My parents had decided before they were married that four children would comprise the perfect family, and so we arrived, one boy and three girls. Later my dad would say that he had one girl to wash the dishes, one girl to dry the dishes and the other one to put away! We honestly believed this was the case until many years later. My mom, on the other hand, believed God gave her three daughters to help her take care of my dad! Whatever the case may be, looking back now, my brother, two sisters and I feel very privileged to have been a part of our family. God allowed us the opportunity to serve our parents in a way that many do not experience, especially as young adults.

It was a warm and beautiful September afternoon when I attended a medical appointment with Mom. We were hoping for some proactive treatment for a nagging foot problem she had been experiencing on her left side for a year. We had come to hear the treatment plan from the neurosurgeon. Mom was nervous but hopeful; she had never been keen on going to medical appointments.

When the doctor entered the room he examined Mom as he had done before, left the room briefly and came back with his notes, a drinking straw and an elastic band. He quickly began to summarize the procedures my mom had been through and was reporting the finding as ALS (Lou Gehrig's disease). I will never forget the complete look of horror on my mom's face as he spoke those words. Her mother had been diagnosed with ALS when my mom was a young adult. As a result, my grandmother spent 11 years in the hospital being treated for ALS. At that time, Mom had been informed by my grandmother's doctor that she did not need to fear getting this disease as it is not inheritable.

Mom attempted to explain this to the neurosurgeon when he informed us that there is a Familial ALS and perhaps her children should consider getting tested. As the doctor prepared to explain about the disease using the drinking straw and elastic band, I quietly told him that, unfortunately, we were already more than well aware of the horrors of the disease, and did not have any questions. He nodded his head and had tears in his eyes.

We left the room and I held Mom as we walked the hallway of the hospital. I was in shock but felt I should sing to her a song we sang in church in which the lines say,

"Whose report will you believe? We shall believe the report of the Lord!" I felt the fear of what was going to happen cover me like a cloud. Mom was sobbing as we drove home, concerned about how Dad would handle the news. Ever the caretaker and loving wife, she wanted to make sure we got home quickly so she would be there in time to prepare his supper. As we arrived home, the rest of the family had assembled on the porch to wait for the news. My dad was anticipating some type of treatment that would assist my mom and all would be well.

> "As the doctor prepared to explain about the disease…I quietly told him that unfortunately we were already more than well aware of the horrors of the disease."

Mom got out of the car and sank into my dad's arms. She whispered the news and my dad began to pray. My brother and sisters were devastated and shocked. However, we believed that God is sovereign and only He could change the impossible and heal my mom.

ALS or Amyotrophic Lateral Sclerosis is a disease, in which the myelin sheath which covers the nerves is destroyed. Thus, the nerves become like a frayed electrical wire unable to send the proper messages to the body. If you picture the myelin sheath as a plastic drinking straw and the nerve as the elastic band you can appreciate the visual image. There have been no found drugs to date to slow down or assist ALS sufferers; none that have been available for treatment, outside of some clinical trials. As a result of this disease an individual has a life expectancy of one to three years on average. The progression of this disease depends on the individual or type. It affects the movement of the arms and legs, the neck, the ability to speak, eat and swallow. Eventually, it causes respiratory complications as individuals are no longer able to breath on their own. There is no known cause for ALS and it is often sporadic. It may run in families and genetic testing may identify the gene. However, there is no certainty that if you have the gene you will get the disease.

I am blessed to have come from a family who believes in God. We each have a personal relationship with Jesus Christ. Although there have been many times that we could not see the purpose or understand why, we know that God cares and loves us. We live in a world "where the rain falls on the just and the unjust" (Matthew 5:45), yet my family chose to trust in God and it was not easy!

"Dad, a quiet man who didn't usually show a lot of emotion, began to cry. I knew it was not for himself he was crying, but for us."

Fortunately, my mom, who loved to sew, was able to quilt and do hand sewing. She also enjoyed the ability to go online and take care of the household finances, and delegate many of her previous responsibilities. Slowly but surely she lost the ability to walk, to talk clearly and she had choking problems when she would eat or drink. My sisters and I assumed her personal care responsibilities and felt very blessed to help our mom. It was very humbling for her but she remained cheerful and appreciative, never losing faith that God loved and cared for her and that He could heal her broken body.

It was about a year and a half after Mom's diagnosis that my dad began to experience abdominal problems. He became concerned and went to the doctor to find out what could be done to alleviate his discomfort. It was explained to my dad that he had a blockage in his bowel and needed to get to the hospital immediately. As I drove to the hospital I prayed that this would just be a simple procedure and all would be well. I was concerned since I had never seen my dad in pain like this. After hours in the emergency room and multiple painful tests and exams, Dad was sedated as he waited for the surgeon to do a colonoscopy the next morning. Dad requested that I attend the examination with him so I sat beside him and held his hand. As the surgeon performed the procedure with all grace and modesty, he showed my dad the T.V. screen so he could see the growth of the tumour that was blocking his bowel. Dad, a quiet man who didn't usually show a lot of emotion, began to cry. I knew it was not for himself he was crying, but for us.

After surgery it was confirmed. My dad was diagnosed with colon cancer and twenty-six of his lymph nodes also had cancer in them. It was decided that he would receive chemotherapy and radiation treatment. After a family meeting it was decided that one of the girls would need to stay home to assist Dad and Mom. It was determined that

> "Having both of your parents ill with the possibility of knowing they could die can take your breath away."

Megan, their youngest daughter, would be the ideal person. It was with wonderful love and grace that Megan would attend to their needs; packing my dad's wound, assisting with walking, transporting and doing whatever else was needed to help them be comfortable.

It was only God's strength that showed us how to get through this time. Having both of your parents ill with the possibility of knowing they could die can take your breath away. People would often ask how we did it, and we would respond, "We take it one minute at a time, anything else is too much. God is our strength."

After six months of treatment Dad was given a clean bill of health and told to go on with the rest of his life! We were so excited and gave praise to God.

Mom was a strong and faithful mother and wife. She had been weakening a bit but enjoyed getting out to Starbucks to have her caramel macchiato once a day and we enjoyed taking her. On October 18, 2003 I went early in the morning to have some wisdom teeth taken out. My dad and sister, Nancy, accompanied me. I had kissed Mom goodbye and she hugged and prayed for me before I left since I was anxious about the procedure. When we arrived home later that morning my mom and sister were resting in the family room and I didn't want to disturb them. I went up to my room to lie down, only to hear my sister Nancy screaming a few minutes later, "Mom, Mom answer me... don't do this to me Mom..." I ran downstairs with my mouth filled with freezing and gauze. "Call 911 and start CPR," I screamed and ran to let my dad know. He cried, "call 911" and came inside. Minutes later the ambulance was there. Mom still had a pulse and was being taken to the hospital. Dad told me to stay home, as he was concerned I was not well enough to come. I watched from the window, my dear mom being put into the ambulance.

I did not realize that would be the last time I would see her. Later on at the hospital Dad made the decision that she would not be put on the ventilator.

My dad and sisters said their painful goodbyes, and Mom passed away peacefully; "*absent from the body but present with the Lord*" (2 Corinthians 5:8). My mom's death was very painful to our family. We believe that God can heal and we know that He is sovereign. We didn't know why the love of my dad's life was no longer on this earth to care for and love him. What we did know was that we could love and trust that God is faithful even when we don't see what we want or expect should happen.

As we walked through this time of sorrow, we were ever more grateful that my dad was well. He continued working at his sheet metal trade and was trying to adjust to his new life without his true love. He would say that according to him he was still married to my mom, they were just parted by death. In June of 2004 I married my dear husband. It was a joyful time mixed with sorrow as a daughter needs her mom during these times in life. Shortly after my wedding, Dad had a medical appointment which again pronounced him all clear!! We were so happy to have our healthy dad.

> "I truly was not sure if I could go through this again;"

A few months after our wedding my husband and I were pleased to let my dad know that we were expecting our first child, and he was to be a grandpa. Needless to say, Dad was excited and joyful, awaiting the new arrival.

In late November of 2004 Dad began to experience some discomfort in his abdomen, and felt he should get it checked out to see if there was a muscle pulled. He went to the doctor and had a normal course of tests to check up on this situation. As we attended the follow up appointment to hear the results, we were hoping it was a simple issue. We were about to be floored by the results.

My father learned that the cancer in his colon had spread to his liver and lungs. This time the cancer was terminal and it was recommended that he seek palliative care, chemotherapy and/or radiation.

We sat there with our mouths open. We could not believe the news. Dad asked how much time he had and the doctor responded, "anywhere from six months to a year." All we could think was "how could this be?" We were in a complete fog and devastated. I truly was not sure I could go through this again; it was only fair to have at least one parent, I thought.

Certainly God would heal and spare my family from more grief. Dad sought out various forms of treatment but all made him very sick and he lost a lot of weight. He finally decided he would choose to enjoy his time and put his faith in God for the outcome. I remember talking to him and saying, "whatever happens, Dad, you win." He agreed. Either he would be healed and live to be with his family or he would pass away and live in heaven where he could be with my mom.

On March 6, 2005 the awaited grandchild was born five weeks early, but healthy and strong! I was so grateful to allow my dad the privilege of being a grandpa. Dad experienced great joy from the birth of his grandson, and he could be cheered up by him when nothing else would do the trick.

During a full year of deteriorating health, Dad was lovingly cared for by all of his girls. It was a great privilege and a joy to care for him; he was a very kind, quiet and humble man who deeply loved God and his family. He never blamed God for his circumstances. However, he could not help but be concerned for his children, whom although he considered young adults, were still too young to be without parents.

> "He never blamed God for his circumstances."

On March 7, 2006 the day after his grandson's first birthday my dad went home to be with his Lord, surrounded by his girls who were able to care for him at home until his last breath. It was very difficult, as we knew he had tried so hard to stay with us on this earth. We have great comfort in knowing we will see him again in heaven because we have accepted Jesus Christ into our hearts and we know that there is a place prepared for us in heaven (John 14:1-3). There are still days of sadness and sorrow, and we will always miss our parents. We are grateful for their legacy and what their lives have taught us. It is engraved on their headstone, "In God I put my trust." We know that whatever the circumstances, God is faithful and He can be trusted.

Dan's Story

I was raised in a dysfunctional family with both parents being alcoholics. My father never paid much attention to me, if any, either drunk or sober. My mother was not much better, although she somehow managed to stay sober a few days of the week. Looking back now I would say that I was neither shown nor given any love. When they both drank I could be sure of a horrible fight between the two of them when they came home from the hotel. I would be awakened from a deep sleep by my mom's blood curdling screams because of my dad beating her. This was routine just about every night for years. I believe it was the start of my depression, although at the age of eight I had no idea why I felt the way I did.

> "By the time I was twenty-nine years old I was sick and tired of drinking."

Life went on and I found it hard to concentrate in school. I lost interest in many other activities. By the time I was ten, whenever I saw my mother preparing to go out, I knew what that meant; I would have to listen to another night of beatings and I would be wondering again if maybe he would kill her. Just before she would leave I would tell her that I would never drink or smoke when I grew up, and she'd just laugh and say, "yes you will." I didn't know it at the time, but she was right.

By the time I was fifteen and in high school I began drinking, mostly just on the weekends at parties with older friends from school. I liked the way alcohol made me feel. It seemed to lift the heaviness and depression off me, that I now believe I'd had since I was four years old. I left high school in grade ten and was married the following year at the age of seventeen. The years went by and I continued to drink more and more each and every day. I never paid much attention to my family and was somewhat like my parents, except for the fact that I never beat my wife or children.

Then one Sunday morning after a heavy night of drinking until three A.M., I came down, turned on the TV and on the screen there was a TV Evangelist. He pointed his finger at me and said, "you mister who has been out all night drinking and you're all sick and hung over, I've got a message for you. God loves YOU." I felt something change inside me. I'd never heard those words expressed to me that way before. I began to watch every Sunday, for years, because I wanted to learn about this God and His love.

Faithfully, I watched that evangelist preach on TV every Sunday morning, still sick and hung over from all the drinking. By the time I was twenty-nine years old I was sick and tired of drinking. I was getting more and more depressed and now drinking was fuelling the depression. I wanted so desperately to stop, but I was powerless. One night while drinking at home, near the end of the night, I asked my wife, "why doesn't God take this drinking addiction away?" She replied, "we'll have to pray for that." She did pray but I still found myself drinking and feeling worse than ever.

However, in 1992 at the age of thirty-five things were about to change. It would be nothing for me to sit down and drink twenty-five or thirty bottles of beer in a night. I was at my worst; I felt I was in a dark pil of hell. The depression was so terrible that I could not sleep. I hardly ate; I wanted nothing to do with anyone anymore. I had a constant heart rate of well over a hundred at all times. I really did feel I was going to die if nothing changed. To tell you the truth, the way I felt I really didn't care if I did die. I felt there was nothing left, my hopes, dreams and ambitions were all taken away by the alcohol.

> "The chains that had held me a prisoner for over twenty years were broken. . ."

On October 7, 1992 my brother called and wanted me to go out drinking. We went to a bar I'd never been in before. While sitting at the bar ordering our fourth or fifth drink, a lady came up to the bar and stood beside my brother. He asked her if he could buy her a drink. She came over to me, looked me right in the eyes and said "I used to drink but I don't anymore. I'm an angel, do you believe me?" I hadn't laughed so loud in a long time and I told my brother, "this broad is nuts!" Then she looked at me again and repeated the exact same words. "I used to drink but I don't anymore. I'm an angel, do you believe me?" I looked at her for a few minutes and said, "yes, I believe you." The moment I said "yes" something changed, I could feel it instantly. I left my drink and phoned my wife to come and pick me up. I told her that I wanted to go home now; she said "already, you just got there?" I replied, "I'll tell you all about it when I get home."

We arrived home early that Friday night, which was very unusual. As I was telling my wife about what took place in the bar, I opened up all the beers I had at home and poured them down the sink. I believe she was in shock to hear the words I had just spoken and was especially shocked to see me dump out a dozen or more beers. I knew in my heart I would never drink again. However, I'm not so sure that she knew it.

Twenty years of drinking had ended in an instant. I don't know if the woman that night was an angel or not. I do know this – God used that person to say those words to me to change my life in an instant. The chains that had held me a prisoner for over twenty years were broken and I was set free by the grace of God!

That was sixteen years ago and I have never had any desire at all for alcohol in those sixteen years. And yes, the depression was lifted as well. Family life and relationships are restored too. The one thing I've learned from all this is that nothing is impossible for God. If He did it for me, He'll do it for you.

God Bless

Evelyn's Story

As a middle child in a very loving Manitoba home, from my earliest recollections, I remember the laughter and singing. Every Sunday my mother would be sure that we were all dressed in our best clothes and would be at our most attentive behaviour during the service at the Ukrainian Catholic Church. During the Christmas season, my parents taught us to sing beautiful Christmas carols in Ukrainian. We went to catechism, were taught the Ten Commandments and learned that God is always watching over us. After my first communion, I tried not to sin, so that I wouldn't have to tell the priest about it at my next confession.

After finishing high school and teaching for one year in a country school, I went to the University of Manitoba in Winnipeg. Later I attended Teacher's College in Toronto and then taught elementary school in Oakville, Ontario. Amazing things happened during this period of my life. One day I met a wonderful man on the elevator. We both lived in the same apartment building on different floors. We spoke briefly. The following weekend we met again. This is the man I later married. We were extremely happy with an excellent, loving marriage, two beautiful children and a lot of laughter.

When our son was about one year old I bought my first Bible, eager to read it, but found it very difficult to understand. About a year later I attended a gathering called 'Camp Farthest Out'. My husband could not go due to his work schedule so I went with our children and his parents. We listened to teachers, heard personal testimonies, and attended Bible studies and times of singing when jubilant people clapped their hands. I became aware of how joyful and loving these folks were. It was clear to me that they knew Jesus so much better than I did. I wanted that closeness to Him, too.

I learned how Jesus wants to have a close relationship with us. I could have this intimacy too if I confessed my sins to God and asked Jesus to come into my heart. I had thought that I already was a Christian. I had gone to church since I was a young girl and had tried to live a good life. Now for the first time I totally understood that Jesus died for me. However, I had never personally invited Him to come into my heart. More than anything, I wanted to know Jesus the way these people did! On August 21, 1977, I gave my life to Jesus and He became my personal Lord and Saviour. The Holy Spirit, whom I hadn't known before, became my constant companion and teacher.

My husband could see the change in me as I excitedly told him all that had transpired. I began a Bible study right away. I loved learning from the Bible and from my new Christian friends, sharing what I learned with my husband. We were invited to go to a church in Mississauga which soon became our church home.

About a year after I gave my life to the Lord, our whole family attended a weekend retreat where my husband went forward to receive Christ as his Saviour. Shortly afterward, we were both baptized in water. In the following few years, both of our children followed this path. It was a wonderful time of spiritual growth for our whole family. We were so grateful to God for all His wonderful blessings to us.

In 1985 we were transferred to London and our pastor from Mississauga suggested that we attend the LGT Family Church. We continually sought to grow spiritually at church and in Bible studies. However, in one and a half years, my husband received another job transfer, so we were relocated to Kentucky. It was an exciting time but one and a half years later, we were transferred again.

"We all felt like we were the happiest family, living the perfect life!"

When we arrived in Virginia Beach, we felt very happy that maybe we would settle here. My husband felt that we should begin the process to get a more permanent status for living in the States, as we were still all here as Canadian citizens on his work visa. We lived in a lovely condo overlooking the ocean during the construction of our new home, and finally in August our new home was ready. We were very happy here! Our children, now 13 and 14, loved the beach and my husband and I enjoyed our new church, our new neighbours, and making the adjustments to his new work and the beautiful area in which we now lived. We all felt like we were the happiest family, living the perfect life!

I started a prayer group at my home, where several ladies met once a week, and we all became very close friends, as we prayed for one another, our families and friends, and all our concerns. God was so faithful in answering our prayers! I felt that I had very few prayer requests, but mostly just praise for the Lord, as God had blessed us in every way. In fact, I remember thinking that living the Christian life was not difficult at all.

Then my life took a very sudden turn. The day after Christmas, my husband went jogging which he did quite regularly. This time, however, was different. He had been gone for more than half an hour. Expecting him to return, I looked out the window to see if I could see him. I did see him, lying on the road just a few feet from our driveway. I awoke the children and we all ran outside. One of the neighbours must have called an ambulance as it arrived almost immediately. They quickly checked my husband.

> "The love of my life, my life partner was gone. It was like someone erased him from the world!"

Nothing else was done except to summon me into the back of the ambulance. There they gave me the news that my husband was dead. This was unbelievable! I walked over to my husband and crouching over his lifeless body, I looked up, asking God, "what now, Lord?" My mind could not accept this information. My thoughts were spinning, my mind confused. The love of my life, my life partner, was gone. It was like someone erased him from the world. Less than an hour ago we had been planning a fun day. It was too much to comprehend.

I had not even accepted the fact that my wonderful husband had died when the ambulance driver wanted to know where to take his body, where the funeral would be held, and where he would be buried. Who could know this? At our age we hadn't even discussed such topics. We had planned to get old together and 'live happily ever after'! All I could do was pray and cry. God reminded me that He was taking care of me.

They took his body to a nearby funeral home. A man working there had previously worked in a Canadian funeral home in Oakville, the city where we met, got married, and where both of our children were born. It was clear which funeral home to use and the pastor from Mississauga agreed to do the service. Somehow, with God's help, these things were all arranged. My mind was unclear, but even so, I decided he would be buried near his mother, who had passed away about ten years earlier. God confirmed this was the correct decision when the only plot available was numbered the same as the address number of our home. I was reassured that I was on the right track.

I felt so fragile, like I could break, or perish totally, but I needed to be strong for my children. Life was not easy now. The love of my life was gone. His clothes and our wonderful memories were all I had left. I am sure that God carried me through the days and weeks that followed. I cried daily and couldn't sleep. My children were concerned about me. My friends and family were prayerful and supportive, but there were things that were just so very difficult. We were Canadians living in the USA and the government issues were huge. My nights were horrible as I tried to find answers to my new questions. I felt the heavy load of my new responsibilities.

> "Peace settled into my heart and we became excited to see where God wanted us to live."

After the children finished their school year we would be moving back to Canada. One of my concerns was where we would live. Day after day I prayed and cried out to God for direction and guidance. I heard nothing from God at that time, which really troubled me. As I look back, though, God was at work and soon He would show me our future home.

During the spring break, I took the children to Canada to search for our new home so that it would be there for us when we moved at the end of June. Peace settled into my heart and we became excited to see where God wanted us to live.

I had contacted realtors in Mississauga, Oakville, and London, since we had friends in these cities. We loved the fellowship with the Mississauga church and the LGT Family Church. Attending a good church was important to us. When we met with the real estate agents, the answer was the same in both Mississauga and Oakville; no homes were available that would fit our needs. It was very clear that the home we were to have was not in either of these two cities, so we drove to London. It was Tuesday afternoon when we arrived and registered at our hotel. Our realtor was very apologetic since the list of potential homes wasn't long. The market was brisk and homes were selling quickly. The children and I knew that we had definite direction as to what was not the right home, but we hadn't found the one that was the correct home for us yet. Strangely, we weren't panicking and we hadn't lost our excitement in anticipation. We knew that we needed to find our home in this week, and so we just continued to pray and believe that it would be shown to us.

How did we know the exact house where we should live? It was perfectly clear! There was only one house in the area we liked that met the needs of our family, which was the size we needed, and at the right stage of construction. There was only one problem. The builder had told the realtor that he would not sell the house since he was building this one to be his model home. It was at the framing stage and there was no other home that even came close to what we would consider buying. We convinced the realtor to write up an offer and present it to the builder. Our week for our home search was almost finished. The builder was sick at home, but by noon he accepted my offer. Now we knew what home God chose for us! We spent Friday afternoon making all the selections; the flooring, brick, kitchen cupboards, bathroom vanities, lighting, door and hardware choices, all the paint colours throughout the house, and the locates for the electrical and cable receptacles. A job normally scheduled over a period of weeks was done in a day. We did not return to see the construction of our home but trusted that God would watch over it. With one day left before our flight back to Virginia Beach, I spent it buying my car. That too would be ready for us when we returned in three months. As we left Canada I had peace in my heart regarding our choices and knew that we had done what was necessary to start our new life without a husband and dad. Slowly we began to make arrangements for this big move.

When we settled into our new home, God provided us with friends and our church was wonderfully supportive. It helped me to know that our pastor knew my hurt and that he prayed for us. Our children were in the church

"When life gets too hard, I know that God never leaves us!"

youth group and very often these teenagers came over to our home after church. I taught fitness classes at the church and later taught a Bible study group at our house. I missed my husband terribly and cried often when I felt lonely. I seemed to notice happy couples everywhere I went and felt stuck in my grief.

My children adjusted well and finished high school. They then went on to college and university. Our daughter married a wonderful man and they now have three beautiful children. Our son, who now is married, has lived in the states for the past ten years. I am so happy that our whole family loves the Lord and wonder sometimes, if we hadn't moved back here, would my children be happily married now? Perhaps I'll never know why their dad's life was so short, but we do know that we will see him again one day.

My own life is so different now. I have remarried and work full time. My husband and I read the Bible together daily and we continually seek God's direction for our lives. We live in the same house to which I was directed almost twenty years ago. We love our Christian friends and get together with our children and grandchildren as often as possible. As we approach our retirement years, we wonder what God has planned for us. Our life is in His hands. Since we know that our steps are ordered by the Lord, we don't fear what's ahead. God is faithful. Having been a Christian now for over thirty years, I know that I can trust God through everything. When life gets too hard, I know that God never leaves us. In getting through my difficulties, I learned things about God and myself that I would normally not know. I am so grateful that I have Him in my life.

<u>John's Story (Evelyn's husband)</u>

Prior to July 1991 my life was not settled. I was in debt, had high blood pressure, and was socializing with secular people. One day I was introduced to a wonderful woman who was a Christian with outstanding qualities. That's when my life started to change. A month after I met her, this lovely lady led me to the Lord.

Up to that point in my life I had no Christian friends and also had never known any Christian people. I started attending church immediately and began to notice a significant change in my health. My self esteem improved and I was now beginning to get involved within the church. The very next year I married this lovely lady who had led me to the Lord. I have been blessed every single day since, not only by having her in my new life but also by having the Lord in my life as well.

As the years went on I was diagnosed with having cancer which was a traumatic experience for both of us. With prayer and faith my wife and I were able to overcome the news of this terrible tragedy. Later on, arthritis set into my body which has slowed me down somewhat. However, my faith in what the Lord is doing and what will be done keeps me going day by day.

I know that, someday, either on earth or in heaven, all will be well and all pain will be removed. Without the love and prayers that come from my wife, my journey would indeed be a difficult one, maybe even impossible. Through prayer, faith, and believing in the Lord Jesus Christ all things are possible.

Ervis and Tamara's Story

There are always childhood anecdotes to tell, but this little Cuban boy treasured a lovely one in his heart. Every day on his journey to buy milk for his mother, he passed by the house of a little girl with two big pony tails. She was always at the front of the house where she lived with her two brothers and parents. Even though they had never spoken, and besides the fact that he was only eight years old, there was something captivating every time he saw her. Then his family moved to another town and he was not able to continue seeing her every day.

At the age of fifteen, Ervis moved back to his former community in Cuba to attend high school. When he entered his classroom for the first time, there she was, Tamara, the girl with the pony tails. Now she was an enchanting teenager. She was quite surprised when this boy saw her and said he recognized her from his childhood. They had a beautiful relationship for three years, but a bad decision made him end it, which broke her heart. Eight years passed and during this time Ervis never forgot the girl with the pony tails.

One day while Tamara's father was in the hospital dying, Ervis was completing his internship as a doctor in the same hospital. When Ervis saw Tamara, the only words he spoke to her were, "I am here for you." And so he was. A while after Tamara's father died, she and Ervis decided to renew their relationship.

> # He also, as a doctor, was obligated to order abortions which he always refused to do...

In 1994 Ervis became a medical doctor and practiced medicine for some years. It was that same year in October that both Ervis and Tamara experienced spiritual birth. In January of the following year they were married with the blessing of God.

As a young doctor with a new found faith, Ervis was eager to share his hope with some of his patients. He gave them related literature to take home to read. This was not allowed in Cuba so he was confronted by a government official who told him not to do this. He also, as a doctor, was obligated to order abortions which he always refused to do because of his belief that life is sacred from conception. He found it difficult to combine his medical career with his new spiritual life so he made a decision. Ervis notified the director of the clinic that he would no longer work for the clinic but instead he would work for the Lord.

Ervis left his medical career to become a servant of God. Tamara, who graduated from the "Las Villas" university as an interpreter and translator of English, left that very profitable job. Together they followed the same "call " in this amazing journey, a challenge of faith. They were part of the group that founded a church in Placetas, a town in the center of

Cuba. Their ministry developed in this church under very difficult circumstances with very little money. Because the government did not want them to have a church there, they were forced to use a property behind a house in a muddy yard without a roof. For months, their church services were held under a very hot sun, in the rain, and in the evenings, beneath the clear moonlight. It was rough. They did, by faith, go against the government and put a roof on the building, which remains today.

At a church service In 1997 a lady approached Tamara and Ervis telling them she had a dream. In her dream, she saw them at an airport, wearing coats and Tamara was holding a small girl. Little did Tamara and Ervis know that ten years later this lady's dream would become a reality.

> **This seemed like a near impossibility since Ervis had been earning the equivalent of $12 per month as a doctor.**

In 1998 Tamara gave birth to their son, and later in 2003, their daughter. It was January 18, 2007 when the family left Cuba, after thirteen years of serving God there. Yes, Ervis and Tamara were standing in the airport wearing their coats and she was holding her little girl just as in the lady's dream, and their journey to Canada began.

It was not that simple though. A pastor had invited Ervis to preach at a church in Canada. His entry was denied. A man at the embassy explained the process. It would cost $6000 and they were required to have $18,000 on deposit in a Canadian bank. This seemed like a near impossibility since Ervis had been earning the equivalent of $12 per month as a doctor, and subsequently, only $10 per month as a pastor. Where would they get this kind of money?

Tamara's one brother was now living in Miami. A pastor borrowed money for Ervis' family to get their passports. Ervis' sister, also living in Miami, asked what they needed to get to Canada. Her father-in-law gave them $500. Friends in Canada established a Settlement Fund in their names for $18,000, the required amount. The agreement was that they repay it at the rate of $150 per month. This is being covered by a group of Cuban ministers who have pledged to each pay $10 a month over two years. This is a huge stretch for the ministers since their monthly incomes are not a whole lot more than that.

The $6000 that they had to pay to the Cuban Immigration Court at an interview was quite miraculously come by. They prayed and two months later they had the money.

Then there were the tests. They were required to pass a very difficult English exam. Other challenges were the medical tests. Ervis was told he could not travel to Canada because his TB test was positive. Not giving in, he went to the hospital to be retested. This time he tested negative. They experienced increased faith and encouragement through this amazing journey.

The family arrived in Canada and found a home in a town just outside of London close to where they had friends. In their early days in Canada they attended several different churches of various denominations, looking for 'just the right fit'. When they were invited to LGT Family Church, Tamara felt in her heart that they should go. They had not found the right place as yet, but, as Tamara said, "it was amazing! Pastor Bob was so glad to see us! It was awesome! The prayer time was a nice experience and we felt the presence of the Lord." They knew then that it was the church where God wanted them to be. Ervis began procedures with the help of Pastor Bob to get his ministerial credentials for Canada.

> They experienced increased faith and encouragement through this amazing journey.

Life was not without its heartaches. In 2006 one of Tamara's brothers was driving home to Havana with his family and another family when their vehicle became involved in a fatal accident. The members of the other family sustained serious injuries and recovered. However, tragically, Tamara's brother, his wife and two of their three children were killed. Heartbroken, Tamara tried to phone her brother in Miami to inform him of the tragedy. She discovered he was in the hospital undergoing treatment for cancer. He had not told his family.

When living in Cuba this brother had been actively practicing witchcraft and continued to do so in Miami. With her strong faith, Tamara prayed that his soul would be rescued, not that his body would be delivered from despair.

Her prayers were heard and answered. In his hospital bed her brother was given a new life. He was released from hospital and lived another two years.

In that time he and his wife traveled to his home town, Placetas, to share of his new found hope with those he knew. He had not seen his mother for eight years, and there she was, greatly rejoicing. He and his wife then returned to Miami.

Tamara was given permission to travel to the United States on April 18, 2008. She went to Miami to see her brother for the last time, a week before his body succumbed to the cancer. She had lost her father, both of her brothers and two nephews, but she must carry on with her husband and children.

Having been a fully trained and qualified doctor in Cuba, then a credentialed minister of a church, Ervis, a new Canadian, is now a recent graduate as a certified Personal Support Worker. He has served his internship and will be the most remarkable PSW that anyone in need will experience.

Combined with his recent training, his knowledge as a doctor, and his caring manner, he most certainly has found the place where God wants him at this time. Now living in London with his wife Tamara (the little girl with the two big pony tails) as well as their two beautiful children, they are marching forward in a new life. An opportunity opened for Ervis and Tamara to conduct a Hispanic service and Bible study each week at LGT Family Church.

We do not know what the future holds, but we do know WHO holds the future!

Grace's Story

I remember going to church since the age of two. My life was pretty 'standard'. I had a nice family and nice friends. I was once hurt by a boyfriend but recovered from that broken relationship. I had always been a hard worker and very dedicated to whatever work I was doing. Everything always went very smoothly for me.

I graduated from UWO and Teachers College, eager to set out in my chosen career. I wanted to be the best teacher that I could possibly be.

In my first year of teaching, everything seemed to be great. My co-workers liked me and we had a good rapport. Those in senior administration often stepped into my classroom to observe

> "I felt like I was under attack from an enemy. I cried a lot..."

my teaching and approved of everything I was doing. I was spoken of highly by others. I was confident and did well that year. I had a mixed class, including a few children with behavioural needs, but they respected me and I loved my teaching. The kids at school were not perfect, but they were manageable.

I felt like I was off to a great start my second year of teaching. I had a very challenging group of kids with no class assistant. A big part of the class was made up of children who were emotionally challenged and, as you can imagine, difficult to teach and manage. As well, some children had difficulty with social behaviour. It was in this second year of teaching that everything started to go wrong for me. Even though I was working under the same administration, they no longer seemed to like how I was teaching. There was a lot of criticism directed towards me and it appeared as though nothing I did was ever good enough. I felt like I was hated. In addition, the kids in my class were behaving badly. They were visibly hateful towards me and so were their parents. It seemed like I was under constant oppression, even though, in my opinion, I had done nothing wrong. I felt like I was under attack from an enemy. I cried a lot and was not feeling like myself. I was fighting physically and emotionally. It was draining!

> "I knew that I would have the freedom to work in peace again."

I sought advice from my mom and dad, my mentor and my friends at church. Nothing worked and none of them had any answers for me. My dad told me that I was a hard worker and he was sure everything would be fine. My mentor told me I was doing a great job. No one seemed to understand that everything I was trying was not working out.

It was then that I began to cry out to God. I needed help in every part of my life. I found myself reading the

Bible and praying daily, especially in the early hours of the morning. I would get up at 4:30 or 5:00 in the morning and swallow up the words I was reading. That January, through the Bible verses that I was reading, I saw things that I would never have otherwise understood. I read about people who were in traps, pits and snares. I saw how these things could destroy a person's life. God was speaking to me through the scriptures.

I read about Daniel, a man of strong faith who lived an honest, good life. I read about why and how his enemies threw him into a den of lions to be devoured. I learned about how his strong, unwavering faith put him there and how his strong faith delivered him from the enemy. Mysteriously, the mouths of the lions were shut and he came out unharmed. (Daniel 6:22)

I read about David, the little shepherd boy, who so bravely volunteered to face the giant Goliath. David was mocked by that Philistine but David's faith was strong and he was confident. How miraculously that one little stone he threw from his sling went right to the one vulnerable part of Goliath's body that was unprotected and the giant was defeated! (I Samuel 17:41-49)

Another story that really spoke to me was that of Joseph. When Joseph was in prison, Pharaoh had a dream that someone would be restored back to his original position. I related to the feeling of being held captive, but then also knew that I would have the freedom to work in peace again.

I had a lot of questions and my friends in the Young Adults group at LGT were always supportive and consistently gave the same advice—Keep praying! So I did.

My life began to change. I was attending church regularly, as usual, but now became more focused. The sermons started to make more sense. On Easter weekend of my first year of teaching, I had heard the song 'Jerusalem'. I found it to be quite inspirational. The words spoke to me and made me feel as though it was time to start a new journey. It was incredible! This year it felt like that journey had begun.

In my job I kept trying to improve. It was evident that my co-workers' attitudes began to change. When it was time for my evaluation I didn't want it to be all bad so I began to stand up for myself. Some things were not flawless but I had a good attitude and I knew that I was doing a good job. My evaluation was complete and although it was not perfect, it was better because of the steps I took with confidence.

Now it was time for me to stand back and get a new start. I was young and new at this. I couldn't let the giant destroy me!

I have been blessed this year, my third year of teaching. The parents like me and I feel like I am guided in my teaching. I have more wisdom in what to say and how to treat the kids. They listen to me and like to do their work. They even ask for homework!

I am thankful for God's grace in my life.

Bob's Story

Teary eyes blurred my vision as I guided my blue Chevy north along a California freeway. I cried out to God, "Why do I have to leave my family in our former community and commute to the new church pastorate? I know that I've been called to Bethel Church, San Francisco but why won't our house in Santa Rosa sell?"

Houses were selling. Ours was priced right. Yes, we even reduced the price, and open houses were held weekly. Unexpectedly, between the tears, into my mind's eye came a vision of our real estate agent, Al, with a big smile and a bright yellow shirt open at the collar. It was strange for Al to be wearing an open necked shirt. I had never seen him casually dressed in the three years I had known him. Immediately, I thought I knew what it meant; our house was sold.

When I arrived home I anxiously called our agent. As usual, several people were looking; some were interested but no offers. However, I knew the sale was now ordained of God so we began an earnest search for a San Francisco home. I knew that I was to share on Sunday morning with our new congregation the vision about our agent and his bright yellow shirt.

Needless to say, every week following, people in San Francisco were wondering whether or not Al had worn his yellow shirt yet. As we prepared our priority list for a new house in San Francisco the agent laughed and said that a house like that just didn't exist in our price range. A few weeks later when we found the home meeting more than our list required, at a price we could afford, I knew God was in it. I thought our long possession date would give God lots of time to see our old house sold. After all, isn't this what the walk of faith is all about?

> "One simple question shattered my plan. In life it is good to learn that your spouse is your protection not your challenger."

As weeks rolled into months the answer from our selling agent was always the same, "some interested but no offers." Six months slowly passed and the possession date for our new house was just around the corner.

Two individuals in the church offered to loan us the down payment so we could close the deal on the new house. I thought this was the provision I had been trusting God for. When one of the men took me with him to the bank to arrange an interim loan, the receipts for his government bonds that he planned to use as collateral were the wrong copy. He was told it would take at least a month to send them back to Washington to be re-processed, so he could obtain the corrected copy. Since that would be too late, I moved on to the second man in the church. His visit to the bank was just as unfruitful. His bank manager was on holidays sailing in the Caribbean and the assistant manager had just retired. No one in authority in the bank knew him well enough to authorize the loan. Discouraged and disappointed I returned home.

That night a doctor friend called and asked if we needed Interim financing. He had sufficient funds in a savings account and was willing to loan us the money. I quickly answered "yes" since I didn't want to lose the $10,000 we had put up as down payment. I was only off the phone a few minutes when I told my wife Brenda what his offer was. One simple question shattered my plan. Brenda asked if I felt right at this time in my spirit about accepting the loan from him. In life it is good to learn that your spouse is your protection, not your challenger. The Bible refers to it as "*the Peace of God ruling your heart.*" The answer for both of us was absolutely clear. The next morning I called the doctor and told him I appreciated his offer but would not need his funds. At that moment I knew the only answer was God.

I asked the real estate agent if we could have a twenty-one day extension on the purchase date. The seller came back with a twenty-eight day extension. The real estate agent asked me, "will you have the money in twenty-eight days?"

By faith I answered "yes." I knew I was not to go to any other banks or knock on any doors, but to wait. When I called my real estate agent on the twenty-seventh day and he told me that one person was interested but no firm offers had been made, my heart was racing. I knew that the escrow system in California usually took one or two weeks minimum to close a house sale. The twenty-eighth day of the extension was a warm, sunny day in June. Just after breakfast our selling agent phoned to say he was coming by the house around 11:00 a.m. I saw his car come up the driveway. When he stepped out of the car I knew that what God had shown me through a vision six months before was now a reality. Yes, he was wearing a bright yellow shirt with an open collar! The word of knowledge was true.

Had I told him previously about the vision? No. I didn't want to spoil what God was doing. That day a transaction was processed in record time. By 2:00 p.m. the real estate papers were all signed. The deal went through the lawyers and the money transferred to the San Francisco escrow account by 4:00 p.m.

I know God hears and answers our prayers in His time, but during the process our faith is stretched and human means tested. Like so many spiritual lessons I would not choose to go through it again but I also would not give up what the experience did for me.

To God be the Glory!

Ruth's Story

Many years ago our small town Pastor's wife delivered a sermon challenging us to "ask God for something intangible that you have never asked for before." I was prompted to begin a long journey of prayer for patience.

Some 30 years later, it was pointed out to me that the Bible says "*tribulation brings patience*" (Romans 5:3-5). I knew that scripture. However, through the years I now 'glory in the tribulation'. It has been a huge faith builder and spiritual learning curve for me. I will share a little.

Our first baby was burning up with fever in the middle of the night. Not knowing how to lower a fever, I knew how to pray. As I prayed holding those little, red, hot feet in my hand, I felt them return to normal temperature. As I moved my hand to different parts of his body, the fever left until every part of that little body returned to normal temperature. I thank God for being the Great Physician.

Our young daughter was terminally ill and as I prayed constantly for her healing through buckets of tears, God gave me assurance and hope. I refused to give her up. I wanted her to be well and strong and 'normal'. God sent an angel, an audible voice that I heard say, "she will live." Jesus visited my bedside in the middle of the night and showed me His nail scarred hands. He said, "for you" and then was gone. My faith was strengthened.

Some time after that, our family arrived late to a service at a church we were visiting. The church was crowded but we managed to squeeze into some seats in the balcony. During the sermon the evangelist said, "If you have come here sick and you leave here sick, it's

> "She was never the same. Her illness and weakness were completely gone. I thank God...for her healing..."

your fault, not God's fault." I knew then and there that God would heal our daughter that night. Immediately after the sermon the evangelist pointed directly to our balcony seats and said, "there is someone there with leukemia and I have your healing here". Nobody else at the service went forward for that reason. We sat. He again called out and said, "I still do not have the person with leukemia. I have your healing for you here." It seemed like the healing was something tangible that he was holding in his hand. I prayed that if it was for our daughter, nobody else would go forward to receive that specific healing. Nobody did. Finally after several pleas from him, his worker spotted us and questioned us. When we told her of our daughter's blood and liver condition, she said, "she's the one" and escorted her to the platform. The evangelist prayed for her two times, each time she fell to the floor. I believe that once was for the liver condition and the other for the blood condition. She was never the same. Her illness and weakness were completely gone. Her blood tests were now normal. Because of all the time she had spent in the hospital over the years, she re-chose her occupation. I thank God not only for her healing, but also for directing her path into nursing.

One of our teens was heading for destruction and needed a life turnaround after being dragged into the world of drugs. Our youth pastor prayed on the phone with me, that our son would have a 'supernatural encounter with God'. That is exactly what took place and his life was changed forever.

I thank God that He had the right man in the right place at the right time and He used that man to pray that prayer of faith in our time of need.

Another family event caused me to experience a complete mental breakdown. I learned so much through that experience. I thank God that He changed me and gave me hope. He delivered me from a dependency on medication the doctors said I would have to take for the rest of my life. God led my life in a new direction and enabled me to recapture lost aspirations.

Many times I have prayed for God to provide financially and He has blessed us in some very creative ways. I thank God that He is the Great Provider.

These tribulations have given me more than the reward of patience, at least more than I had 50 years ago. They have given me increased faith and strengthened me. Life is a journey and I still need to use the map (the Bible). "*The Lord is my rock, and my fortress, and my deliverer; my God, my strength, in whom I will trust; my buckler, and the horn of my salvation, and my high tower. I will call upon the Lord, who is worthy to be praised: so shall I be saved from mine enemies*" Psalm 18: 2-3. I know that God is always with us and cares for us.

Joy's Story

Before I trusted Jesus Christ, I was busy in the world, doing all the 'normal' things. I was married with two children, two cars, a house, pets and later a job. I traveled a lot since I had family in two different countries and I wanted to see some of the world. I went to seven different countries which looked great to my friends. However, I was depressed, empty and sad. Nothing made me happy. Something was missing.

> *"...for the first time in my life I had time to figure out what I wanted."*

Finally I decided there had to be something else. I had gone to church as a child but after I got married my husband, who was Roman Catholic, didn't want to go to church. However, my daughter went to a church in our neighbourhood.

Eventually I decided that after everything I had done I still did not feel significant, valuable or purposeful. Since my children were grown up and my now ex-husband was remarried and lived in Montreal, for the first time in my life I had time to figure out what I wanted. I was determined to learn in depth about Jesus, a part of my life that I had neglected.

I can't recall how I found LGT Family Church, but they had activities to keep me busy and out of trouble. By now I had a lot of time on my hands. I could no longer work. I had been in three car accidents within one and a half years. I was side swiped, rear-ended and a drunken driver turned left in front of us when I was a passenger in my friend's car. My memory was affected; I had whip lash, back pain, fibromyalgia, and brain damage. I continue to have memory lapses – I can't focus on a single task. At first I was angry and so unable to call myself disabled.

God gave me a lot of time to really get to know Him. I had decided I was going to put Him first and totally spend my time reading the Bible and doing more productive things.

I went to UWO just so I could call myself a UWO student. I took courses that included both multiple choice and essay questions on the testing. I could do the multiple choice with no problem. Essays were different. I started to see that my thoughts didn't connect sentences. When writing, I would forget the previous sentence so I couldn't get through any essay type tests.

Now, with the help of God's prodding, I resigned myself to depend on Him for all my needs "*according to the riches of His Glory by Christ Jesus*" (Phil. 4:19). By now I was learning who God was. He allowed things to happen but would use all for my good. I learned that He loved me and had a plan to use my gifts and talents for His purpose.

It took approximately fourteen years for God to show me what He wanted me to get and to know. I was learning from the Bible about everything. I used recipe cards and tons of paper, writing down just about everything, so I could remember. Now I am at the point where I say, "Lord if you want me to remember, I'll leave it in Your hands."

Recently, I felt God's urging that I was to join the church choir. I thought, "You must be kidding!" I never for one moment thought I had a voice, so I didn't respond for a year, at least. Each Sunday I would take home the words of songs that were written for that service. I saved the ones that were awesome to me from the very first day at LGT. I never knew why. The songs kept pouring out of me, then I would get stuck and I'd be so frustrated. I wanted to sing!

Finally I felt God's confirmation, "You can do it!" There was a lot happening and God was setting up a scenario for me. Now that I look back, He does what we don't understand even when it looks like a disaster to us, for His plans and our good.

As I grow to know God better, our relationship has become closer. As I read and learn the Bible better, I get to know how He expects me to live and behave. I now realize why He had to take me off the path I was on. For God to actually use me for His purposes, I had to be totally independent of everyone so He could accomplish His will in my life. Now I can see how I make a difference in the lives of the people He brings across my path and I see how Jesus uses me. It is actually funny sometimes when I am helping someone else; I get so much joy and many blessings.

Now God is first in my life. I am aware of the distractions and even people that can take me away from my goal. I am aware that my priority is to please God. I can depend on Him to guide, direct and protect me. There are so many instances of His protection over me.

One day my debit card would not work. I now believe it was because I was not meant to get involved in a multi-level marketing scheme, but I felt pressured and caved in. I checked the card one hour later and it worked and I knew God was there for me again. There have been other times when I got myself into dangerous situations and He has saved me from disasters.

> "Amazingly I was standing about seven feet away from all that broken glass!"

One evening I was finishing hanging a wallpaper border in my living room. As I was stretching to reach over into the corner, I intended to put my toes on the edge of my metal and glass corner table so I could reach the area, but somehow I put my whole foot on the glass shelf. In a flash, everything was on the floor; broken glass from three shelves, the phone, books, everything. Amazingly, I was standing about seven feet away from all of the broken glass! I looked down and saw that my right leg was bleeding. I took a wash cloth and wiped the small amount of blood away and saw seven small nicks that needed Band-Aids. As I thought about it, the enormity of the situation really hit me. It didn't make sense! Who had put me seven feet away from the broken glass? The hole in the shelves measured thirty-four inches; two inches less than my thirty-six inch hips. I would have been stuck if I had gone through the table!

Another incident happened one night when I was leaving the local bank. As I drove across the parking lot, I was unaware there was a three foot drop in my path, protected only by a curb. My car went over the edge of the drop and fell into the deep hole. I remember thinking, "I really can't afford a repair bill at this time," and kept driving. Amazingly, there was no damage to my car and no repairs needed.

> "It's too much for a simple human to understand when we don't have the answers, but God does."

On an overnight visit to a friend's house out of town, as I lay in bed I was unable to fall asleep. I felt like someone was sitting on the edge of the bed, stroking my hair and saying, "All is forgiven. All the things you did wrong in the past, it's all forgiven. I died on the cross to set you free from all guilt and shame." I felt so much love, reassurance and confidence that I truly am valuable and precious to God, and that's all that matters.

Today I am happier than I can ever remember being in my life. I can stay alone at home and not feel lonely. I feel confident, self assured and truly loved by God. I focus on pleasing Him and at the same time remembering I can't do anything without Him helping me as He has all these years. It is just like His promise "*I am the* vine, *you are the branches without Me you can do nothing*" (John 15:5).

I truly know what God means and I know He's true. It makes my life so simple now, knowing I have all the help I need in all areas of my life, big or small. I have "*cast all my cares on Him*" (1 Peter 5:7). We were not meant to worry about tomorrow.

It's too much for a simple human to understand when we don't have the answers, but God does. Now it makes sense to me. My life is easy. I have a partner, one who keeps all His promises, never lies, and is never too tired and never sleeps. He supplies me with supernatural power to get up out of bed earlier than I have ever been able to do. He has enabled me to do all the impossible things. He called me to sing in the choir and to help other disabled people. I am at peace and I have joy in all circumstances. When I get a so-called disaster I quickly hand it over to Him, my everything. I am presently on no medications and I'm enjoying the journey of my life in preparation for my eternity with God.

To Further Encourage You

So now what?

Our hope is that your life can be transformed, just as the people in this book have experienced the life-changing power of God.

Who is God?

The Bible tells us He is POWERFUL. Know that this power is available to YOU! Scripture says He can heal our diseases, control circumstances and release us from problems that have controlled us for years. The stories you have just read prove that. But God is also PERSONAL. He loves you and wants you to think of Him as your Heavenly Father. You can't do one single thing to make Him love you more. You are His child, and He is going to care for you.

Do you know how to talk to God?

It's easier than you think. People call it 'prayer'. Talk to God in the same way you share with someone you trust. Don't worry about whether or not He likes your choice of words —just talk to Him! He is pleased when you take time to just chat with Him about your life.

How can you get to know God better?

The Bible tells us that every one of us, without exception, has broken the tie God made to us when He created Adam and Eve. We have ALL sinned. Perhaps you have heard people say, "I'm a good person...I try to do the right things." They think that impresses God. It doesn't! You can't do something to make God love you, He already loves you.

What is sin? Why should it matter to me?

Throughout life, we think that it is best for US to run our own lives. But as we know, we all make mistakes—we make choices we regret, create pasts we want to undo, and wish we could erase the memories.

Why is it that we make mistakes? Why is it that we hurt other people, even when we don't wish to hurt them? And certainly, we don't want to hurt ourselves, yet we do.

We were never designed to run our own lives ourselves. God designed our lives to be led by Him. When we choose to run our lives instead of Him, we live in rebellion—hurting ourselves, and others all along the way.

Do you need to be rescued?

The Bible in Luke 19:10 tells us, *"For the Son of Man (Jesus) came to seek and to save what was lost."* We were being lost in our sin, He came just in time to save us. We have so much to be grateful for! But God doesn't intend to become JUST your "Saviour". At the exact moment He saves you, you are giving ownership over to Him. Jesus gave His life on the cross to save you and me. As you meet Him at the Cross, it will cost you YOUR life—it is no longer yours! You will no longer live for yourself, but you live your life for Him.

It is as simple as saying this prayer:

"Jesus, I know that I am a sinner. The choice is mine and I choose to give my all to you. I know that I can trust you with my life."

Now that you have taken that step:

God's presence is within you! You will never be alone again! You can share your greatest joys and happiness, but also your greatest pains and problems—and He will carry them all with you!

It's important now to get connected.

You have now become a part of a larger spiritual family. It is vital that you connect with them because God did not intend for you to do this journey alone. God often helps us grow through each other.

If you want to connect with others at LGT Family Church, we welcome you. You can start by visiting one of the programs we have mentioned in this book. Together we can GROW!

Where can I find help and get connected?

There are many groups at LGT Family Church to help you.

▶ **Celebrate Life!** - a women's cancer survivors group that meets monthly

▶ **Dealing with Diabetes and Lifestyle Modifications** - a team of professionals who help individuals and families pursue a healthier lifestyle, including a balanced diet, physical exercise regime and overall better quality of life

▶ **Still Waters** - a weekly group meeting open to men and women desiring to get victory over issues that place limitations on their lives including: Past Trauma, Sexual Abuse, Depression, Fear, Worry or Anxiety, Rejection, Low Self Esteem, Bipolar Disorder, Fibromyalgia or Physical Challenges

▶ **Mom and Me** - an informal weekly gathering for moms with children under 4 years old, to get support and encouragement from other moms

▶ **At The Master's Feet** - a weekly women's group which offers a warm and welcoming environment to grow in the knowledge of God's word, in relationship to Christ and in fellowship with other believers, offering video series and live teaching on different topics relating to spiritual growth

- **R.E.A.C.H for Men** - a weekly addiction recovery group for men
- **Prayer team** - Pastors and spiritual leaders are available to pray with you following every Sunday service
- **Prayer Room** - our prayer room is open during hours the church is open, you can spend quiet time alone talking with God in a peaceful environment
- **Programs for Children, Juniour High, Youth and Young Adults** - contact LGT for more details

Other sources for help:

The Bible is a wonderful resource for some of life's big questions and problems. If you don't have a Bible and would like a copy of The New Testament, please contact our office at 519-685-1920 and we would be happy to provide you with a copy.

Here's some websites that may offer some insight:

www.christiananswers.net
www.crossroads.ca
www.livingfree.com
www.christianrecovery.com

www.mhnet.org
www.drgrantmullen.com
www.christianadvice.net
www.lgt.org

Weekly Services and Programs

You are welcome to join us at any of
our regular **Sunday services:**

9:15 am
11:00 am
2:30 pm: Hispanic Service
6:30 pm

(Sunday School and Children's Church
at 9:15 and 11:00 am services also)

Monday
7:00 pm: "Ignited" Young Adults Program (ages 18+)
7:00 pm: R.E.A.C.H. Recovery for Men (must register first)

Tuesday
10:00 am: Mom and Me

Wednesday
9:15 am: At The Master's Feet Women's Group
6:30 pm: Wednesday night programs for Children
6:30 pm: Junior High (Grades 6-8)
6:30 pm: English Eh! ESL Teaching
6:45 pm: Video Teaching Series for Adults

Thursday
7:00 pm: Still Waters Support Group and Life Skills Training
7:00 pm: Young Ladies Discipleship Group

Friday
6:30 pm: Hispanic Bible Study
7:30 pm: "Driven" Youth Ministries (ages 13-18)

Saturday
7:00 pm: Prayer Group

**LGT Family Church
288 Commissioners Road West
At the corner of Andover
519-685-1920
info@lgt.org**